THE FAIRIES

A POEM BY

WILLIAM ALLINGHAM

ILLUSTRATED BY

MICHAEL HAGUE

Henry Holt and Company

NEW YORK

Up the airy mountain,
Down the rushy glen,

We daren't go a-hunting
    For fear of little men;

Wee folk, good folk,
　　Trooping all together;
Green jacket, red cap,
　　And white owl's feather!

Down along the rocky shore
Some make their home,
They live on crispy pancakes
Of yellow tide-foam;

Some in the reeds
  Of the black mountain-lake,
With frogs for their watch-dogs,
  All night awake.

High on the hill-top
    The old King sits;
He is now so old and gray
    He's nigh lost his wits.
With a bridge of white mist
    Columbkill he crosses,
On his stately journeys
    From Slieveleague to Rosses;

Or going up with music
    On cold starry nights,
To sup with the Queen
    Of the gay Northern Lights.

They stole little Bridget
    For seven years long;
When she came down again
    Her friends were all gone.

They took her lightly back,
　　Between the night and morrow,
They thought that she was fast asleep,
　　But she was dead with sorrow.

They have kept her ever since
Deep within the lake,
On a bed of flag-leaves,
Watching till she wake.

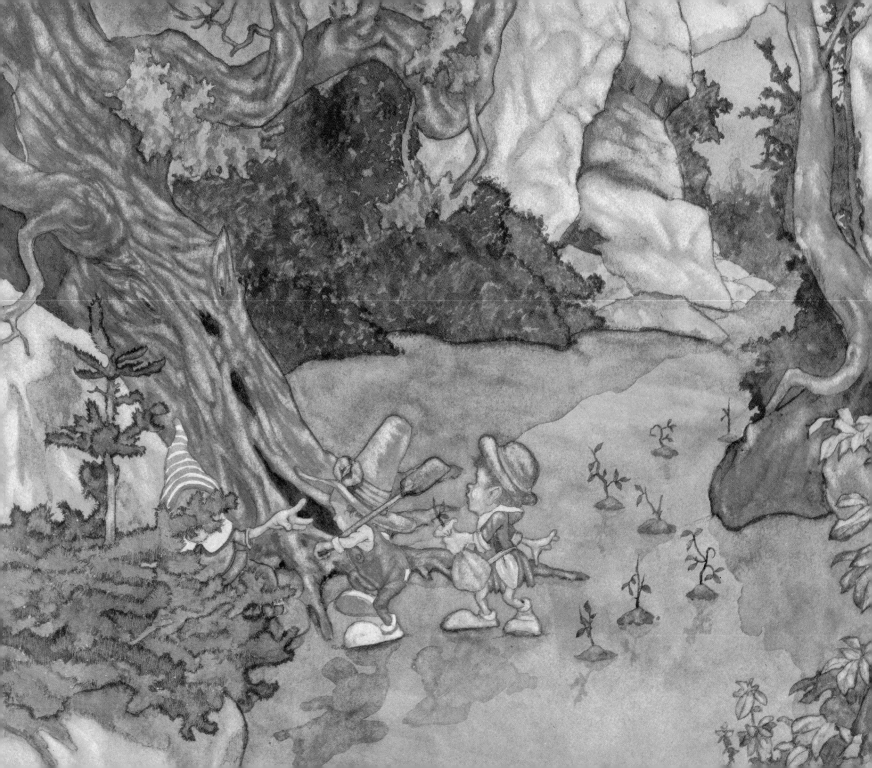

By the craggy hill-side,
    Through the mosses bare,
They have planted thorn-trees
    For pleasure here and there.

Is any man so daring
   As dig them up in spite,

He shall find their sharpest thorns
In his bed at night.

Up the airy mountain,
    Down the rushy glen,
We daren't go a-hunting
    For fear of little men;

Wee folk, good folk,
    Trooping all together;
Green jacket, red cap,
    And white owl's feather!

Published by Henry Holt and Company, Inc., 115 West 18th Street, New York, New York 10011.
Published in Canada by Fitzhenry & Whiteside Limited, 195 Allstate Parkway, Markham, Ontario L3R 4T8.

Library of Congress Cataloging in Publication Data
Allingham, William, 1824–1889. | The fairies.
Summary: An illustrated version of the nineteenth-century poem about the "little men" and the mischief that they do.
1. Fairy poetry, English.   2. Children's poetry, English.   [1. Fairies — Poetry.   2. English poetry]
I. Hague, Michael, ill.   II. Title.   PR4004.A5A626   1989   821′.8   88-28474
ISBN 0-8050-1003-3

First edition | Designed by Marc Cheshire | Printed in the United States of America
1 3 5 7 9 10 8 6 4 2